HEINEMANN
STATE STUDIES

Uniquely
Virginia

Karla Smith

Heinemann Library
Chicago, Illinois

18359701

Designed by Heinemann Library
Page layout by Wilkinson Design
Printed and bound in the United States by Lake
Book Manufacturing, Inc.

07 06 05 04 03
10 9 8 7 6 5 4 3 2 1

**Library of Congress
Cataloging-in-Publication Data**

Smith, Karla, 1947-
    Uniquely Virginia / Karla Smith.
        p. cm. -- (Heinemann state studies)
    Summary: Discusses the symbols, natural and
man-made
  features, history, and other characteristics which
make the state
  of Virginia unique.
    Includes bibliographical references and index.
    ISBN 1-4034-0361-9 -- ISBN 1-4034-0583-2
(pbk.)
    1. Virginia--Juvenile literature.   [1. Virginia.]
I. Title.
. II. Series.
    F226.3.S655 2003
    975.5--dc21

                                    2002153002

Acknowledgments

The author and publishers are grateful to the
following for permission to reproduce copyright
material:

Cover photography by (main) Jack Hollingsworth/
Corbis (L-R) Corbis, Fred J. Eckert, Alex Brandon/
Heinemann Library, Farrell Grehan/Photo
Researchers, Inc.

Title Page (L-R) Bettmann/Corbis, A. J. Russell/
Corbis, Virginia Secretary of State; contents page
(L-R) Alex Brandon/Heinemann Library, Bettmann/
Corbis, Jeremy Woodhouse/PhotoDisc/Getty
Images; pp. 5, 18B, 35 Corbis; p. 6T
www.onemileup.com; pp. 6C, 6B Virginia
Secretary of State; p. 7T Owen Franken/Corbis;
p. 7B Jeremy Woodhouse/PhotoDisc/Getty Images;
p. 8T Bob Jensen/JENSE/Bruce Coleman Inc.; p. 8B
Starke Jett; p. 9T Andrew J. Martinez/Photo
Researchers, Inc.; p. 9B Photri Inc; p. 10T William
and Mary College; p. 10B Richard A. Cooke/
Corbis; p. 11 Photo Researchers, Inc.; p. 12 David
Muench/Corbis; pp. 13, 20T, 23, 29, 38B, 41, 43T
Alex Brandon/Heinemann Library; p. 14 Pierre
Courtois; p. 16T Steve Solum/Bruce Coleman Inc.;
pp.16B, 17, 26 Bettmann/Corbis; p. 20B Dave G.
Houser/Corbis; p. 21 A. J. Russell/Corbis; 24 Dave
Westerman; p. 25 The Richmond Braves; p. 27
Todd Gipstein/Corbis; p. 28T The Barner Theatre;
p. 28B Nik Wheeler/Corbis; p. 30 Smithfield Foods,
Inc.; p. 31 Andrew E. Cook/Heinemann Library;
p. 32 J & L Waldman/Bruce Coleman Inc.; p. 33
Bessie Weber/Virginia State Parks; p. 34 John
Whalen/Northrop Grumman Newport News;
p. 36 Ann & Rob Simpson; p. 38T Richard T.
Nowitz/Corbis; pp. 39B, 42 Buddy Mays/Corbis;
p. 40 Courtesy of the Maritime Museum; p. 43B
Paul A. Souders/Corbis; p. 44T Jack Hollingsworth/
Corbis p. 44B Paul Rocheleau

Photo research by Julie Laffin

Special thanks to Gary Barr for his expert advice on
the series.

Every effort has been made to contact copyright
holders of any material reproduced in this book.
Any omissions will be rectified in subsequent
printings if notice is given to the publisher.

Some words are shown in bold, **like this.**
You can find out what they mean by looking
in the glossary.

Contents

Uniquely Virginia

Lying on the Atlantic coast of the United States, Virginia has many unique features. Something that is unique has special characteristics that are not common anywhere else. For example, Virginia's history is unique. It is the oldest and largest of the thirteen original English colonies. In 1607, English colonists established the first permanent English settlement in America in a colony called Jamestown.

BIRTHPLACE OF THE NATION

In many ways, Virginia is the birthplace of the United States. Its lawmakers set up the first **representative**

Unique Facts about Virginia

- First permanent English colony in America: Jamestown, 1607

- Two oldest Native American reservations in the United States: near Richmond, Mattaponi (1658) and Pamunkey (1677)

- Last battle of the Revolutionary War: Yorktown, 1781

- Only full-length statue of George Washington made while alive: Jean-Antoine Houdon, Richmond, 1796

- Last battle of the Civil War: Petersburg, 1865

- World's largest shipbuilding yard: Newport News Shipbuilding, 1886

- World's largest office building: Pentagon, Arlington, 1943

- World's largest bridge-tunnel complex: Chesapeake Bay Bridge-Tunnel, 1964

Things to See in Virginia

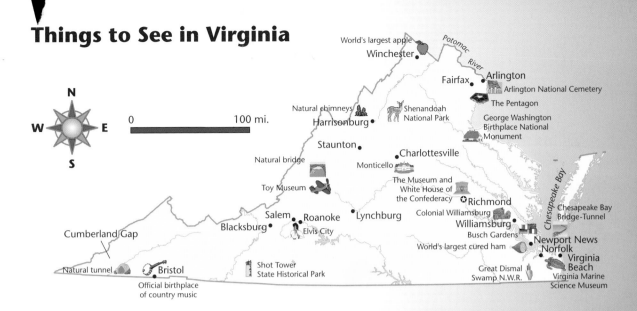

- World's largest apple
- Winchester
- Potomac River
- Fairfax
- Arlington
- Arlington National Cemetery
- The Pentagon
- Natural chimneys
- Shenandoah National Park
- Harrisonburg
- George Washington Birthplace National Monument
- Staunton
- Charlottesville
- Natural bridge
- Monticello
- Toy Museum
- The Museum and White House of the Confederacy
- Richmond
- Chesapeake Bay
- Chesapeake Bay Bridge-Tunnel
- Salem
- Roanoke
- Lynchburg
- Colonial Williamsburg
- Cumberland Gap
- Blacksburg
- Elvis City
- Williamsburg
- Busch Gardens
- World's largest cured ham
- Newport News
- Norfolk
- Natural tunnel
- Bristol
- Shot Tower State Historical Park
- Great Dismal Swamp N.W.R.
- Virginia Beach
- Virginia Marine Science Museum
- Official birthplace of country music

0   100 mi.

government. Four of the first five U.S. presidents were from Virginia. In addition, eight states were formed by western territory once claimed by Virginia. Those states are Illinois, Indiana, Kentucky, Michigan, Minnesota, Ohio, West Virginia, and Wisconsin. Furthermore, Virginia's unique history includes the **Civil War** (1861–1865). More than half of the war's 400-plus battles took place in Virginia. The **Confederacy** also made Richmond its capital, and the Confederacy surrendered in Virginia in 1865. Read on to find out more about all the things that make Virginia a unique, one-of-a-kind place.

Virginia has a range of museums and parks, as well as many places that are important in the history of Virginia and the United States.

Shenandoah National Park's Blue Ridge Mountains form part of the larger Appalachian Mountain chain.

5

Virginia State Symbols

VIRGINIA STATE FLAG

The Virginia state flag contains the front side of the state seal on a blue background.

Virginia adopted its state flag in 1931.

VIRGINIA STATE SEAL

The Great Seal of the Commonwealth of Virginia was adopted in 1931. Virginia based its design on one created in 1776, when Virginia declared independence from Great Britain. The front side of the seal shows the warrior Virtue standing over a defeated **tyrant.** The state motto *Sic Semper Tyrannis* is Latin for Thus Always to Tyrants. The phrase means that tyrants will always be defeated. The reverse side of the Virginia seal shows three Roman goddesses—Liberty, Eternity, and Fruitfulness. Liberty symbolizes freedom, Eternity shows that Virginia will last a long time, and Fruitfulness illustrates **prosperity.** They are standing with a wand, a globe, and a piece of wheat with the Latin word *preseverando,* which means "to preserve" or "to keep."

The fallen tyrant on the top seal is holding a broken chain, symbolizing Virginia's freedom.

The flower of the dogwood tree was selected as the state flower in 1918.

STATE FLOWER AND TREE: AMERICAN DOGWOOD

Virginia selected the flower of the dogwood tree to give people a feeling of pride in their state. The state adopted the dogwood tree as the state tree in 1956. Many Virginians believed that it symbolized the attractive features of Virginia, such as its mountains and rolling hills. The tree's white flowers are some of Virginia's first spring blossoms.

STATE BIRD: CARDINAL

In 1950, Virginia chose the cardinal as its state bird because of its bright feathers and cheerful singing. This bright red bird is a year-round resident of Virginia and can be found throughout the state. The female cardinal has drab-colored feathers to help her blend in with her surroundings. Her coloring helps to make it hard for **predators** to see her.

In England in the 1700s, the cardinal was called the Virginia nightingale.

STATE INSECT: TIGER SWALLOWTAIL BUTTERFLY

In 1991, Virginia adopted the tiger swallowtail butterfly as the state insect. The insect has yellow and black, tiger-striped wings with dark tail-like points. It is one of the most common butterflies in the eastern United States.

The first tiger swallowtail butterflies to be identified in North America came from Virginia.

STATE BOAT: CHESAPEAKE BAY DEADRISE

Not many states have a state boat. The Chesapeake Bay deadrise is a wooden boat made especially for the shallow waters of the Chesapeake Bay and Virginia's rivers. The boat has a tiny cabin and a long deck area, which gives fishers more room to store the day's catch. The boat is perfect for catching crabs and oysters, which live in shallow water. The Chesapeake Bay deadrise was selected as the state boat in 1988.

The deadrise can operate in as little as three feet of water.

State Folklore Center

In 1986, Virginia made the Blue Ridge Institute the State Center for Blue Ridge **Folklore**. The institute hosts the nearly 30-year-old Blue Ridge Folk Festival. The festival includes regional music, food, and a variety of activities, including a mule jumping contest and a horse pull.

STATE SHELL: OYSTER SHELL

The oyster shell is Virginia's state shell because it was an important part of Virginia's seafood business. The oyster was chosen as the state shell in 1974.

STATE DOG: AMERICAN FOX HOUND

George Washington was the first person to breed the American fox hound from an English and a French hound. He raised the dogs for hunting. Most American fox hounds are **descendants** of George Washington's dogs. The American fox hound is, as its name suggests, trained to hunt foxes. Virginia adopted the American fox hound as the state dog in 1966.

Some oysters can live to be more than 50 years of age.

The American fox hound is one of only four dog breeds that were developed in the United States.

STATE FOSSIL: *CHESAPECTEN JEFFERSONIUS*

Virginia adopted the *Chesapecten jeffersonius* as the state **fossil** in 1993. It was the first fossil studied in North America. The fossil's name is taken from Chesapeake Bay, the largest **estuary** in the world.

The fossil was named after Thomas Jefferson because of his interest in natural history.

STATE DANCE: SQUARE DANCE

Virginia adopted the square dance as the state folk dance in 1991. Square dancing is a uniquely American folk dance. It traces its development back to the English country dance and the French ballroom dance.

Square dancers enjoy dancing at one of Virginia's many cultural festivals.

You can identify a brook trout by dark markings on its back, red and whitish spots on its body, and white on the edge of its lower fins.

STATE FISH: BROOK TROUT

In 1993, Virginia's official fish became the brook trout. It is a member of the salmon family. It survives only in clear, cold water. The legislature chose it because it lives in the mountain rivers and streams of Virginia.

STATE QUARTER

The Virginia quarter is the tenth new quarter design to be made by the U.S. Mint. College and university students in Virginia helped choose the picture on the quarter. It shows the three ships that brought colonists to Jamestown in 1607. The ships' names were *Susan Constant, Godspeed,* and *Discovery.*

Virginia became the tenth state in the United States on June 25, 1788.

Commonwealth of Virginia

The title Commonwealth of Virginia was adopted on June 29, 1776. Virginia is one of only four states in the United States officially called a **commonwealth.** Virginia also has an official nickname, which is Old Dominion. King Charles II of England added Virginia to his shield in 1663 because Virginians had remained loyal to him during the English **Civil War** of 1642. France, Ireland, Scotland, and Virginia were his four **dominions.**

Virginia's State Government

Virginia's state government has three main branches—much like the U.S. government. The legislative branch makes the laws. The executive branch carries out the laws. The judicial branch decides how to apply the laws.

LEGISLATIVE

The first General Assembly, or lawmaking body, of Virginia met in Jamestown on July 30, 1619. This was the first **self-government** in the Americas. Virginia has the oldest continuous lawmaking body in North America. Today, the Virginia General Assembly meets in the state **capitol** building in Richmond.

The Jamestown Church was finished in 1647. Its tower is one of the oldest English-built structures still standing in the United States.

The General Assembly is divided into the Senate and the House of **Delegates.** The Senate has 40 members who are elected for a **term** of four years. The **lieutenant governor** is the president of the Senate. The House of Delegates has 100 members who are elected for a term of two years.

*Thomas Jefferson designed the central part of the state capitol. Its **rotunda** contains the only life-size statue of George Washington that he posed for.*

The General Assembly holds regular sessions every year, beginning on the second Wednesday in January. A regular session lasts up to 60 days.

EXECUTIVE

The governor of Virginia is the chief executive of the state. It is the governor's job to make sure that state laws are followed and that the business of the state is carried out. The governor chooses a **cabinet** to help do this. The governor appoints such officials as the treasurer, who keeps track of the state's money. The governor is elected by voters to a term of four years and cannot be elected for two terms in a row. Other members of the executive branch include the attorney general—the state's top lawyer. The attorney general serves a four-year term.

Judicial

The court system of Virginia makes up the judicial branch. It has four levels—the state supreme court, appeals courts, circuit courts, and lower courts. The supreme court is the highest court in Virginia. It has seven **justices,** or judges. They are elected by the General Assembly to serve a **term** of twelve years. The justice who has served the longest on the supreme court is the chief justice for the rest of his or her term.

The next highest court is the court of appeals. It hears cases, such as criminal cases, that people have **appealed** from lower courts. Judges on these courts serve terms of eight years. Circuit court and appeals court judges are elected by the General Assembly. The lower courts of Virginia include juvenile courts and general district courts. The judges in these courts are elected by the General Assembly for terms of six years.

A Symbol of Authority

When the House of **Delegates** is in session, an English-style **mace** is displayed at the front desk of the house chamber. Made in England of silver and 24-carat gold, the mace was presented to the House of Delegates by the Jamestown Foundation. The mace is an age-old symbol of a government's authority.

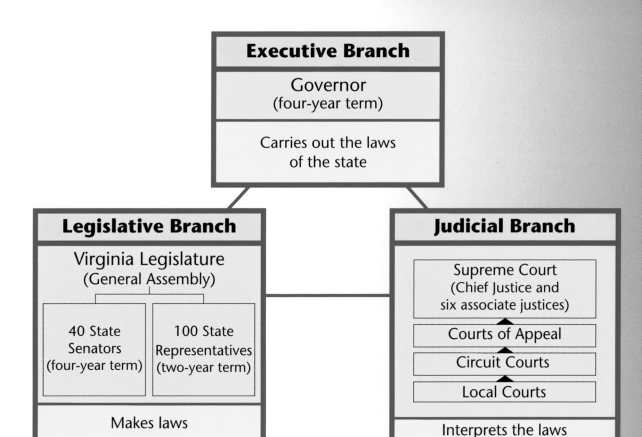

Executive Branch

Governor
(four-year term)

Carries out the laws
of the state

Legislative Branch

Virginia Legislature
(General Assembly)

40 State Senators (four-year term)	100 State Representatives (two-year term)

Makes laws

Judicial Branch

Supreme Court
(Chief Justice and
six associate justices)

Courts of Appeal

Circuit Courts

Local Courts

Interprets the laws

LOCAL GOVERNMENT

A board of supervisors governs all of Virginia's 95 counties except Arlington. Voters elect people to this board to help govern, or run, the county. The board includes such positions as treasurer, sheriff, and county clerk.

Any town with a population of 5,000 or more can do something uniquely Virginian. It can become an independent city that is separate from the county in which it is located. It can even have its own type of government, the council-manager form. In this kind of government, the city council—elected by the voters—performs such tasks as approving and collecting taxes and appointing the city manager. Staunton became the first U.S. city to set up this type of government in 1908. Fairfax, Newport News, and Norfolk are some other independent Virginia cities.

Virginia's state government has three branches—much like the U.S. government.

Birthplace of Many Presidents

GEORGE WASHINGTON

George Washington (1732–1799) is called the Father of Our Country for many reasons. He led the colonies in the **Revolutionary War** as commander-in-chief of the Continental Army from 1775 to 1783. Then in 1791, Washington was elected as the first president of the United States. He served two four-year **terms** and then chose to step down.

THOMAS JEFFERSON

Thomas Jefferson (1743–1826) wanted to be remembered for only three things. They are written on his tombstone:

This statue of George Washington, completed in 1796, stands in Richmond.

Author of the Declaration of Independence

Author of the Virginia Statute for Religious Freedom

Founder of the University of Virginia

Thomas Jefferson was minister to France from 1785 to 1789.

Presidents from Virginia

Name	Birthplace	Term	Order
George Washington	Wakefield	1789–1797	1
Thomas Jefferson	Shadwell	1801–1809	3
James Madison	Port Conway	1809–1817	4
James Monroe	Westmoreland County	1817–1825	5
William Henry Harrison	Berkeley	1841	9
John Tyler	Greenway	1841–1845	10
Zachary Taylor	Montebello	1849–1850	12
Woodrow Wilson	Staunton	1913–1921	28

In 1803, during Jefferson's first term, he bought the Louisiana Territory. It doubled the size of the United States. Thomas Jefferson died on July 4, 1826, exactly 50 years after the **Declaration of Independence** was signed.

JAMES MADISON

James Madison (1751–1836) was a **delegate** for Virginia at the Constitutional Convention in 1787. He was also the main author of the U.S. Constitution. During his presidency, the United States fought in the War of 1812. After the war, he removed troops from the U.S.-Canadian border, which is today the world's longest undefended and unguarded border.

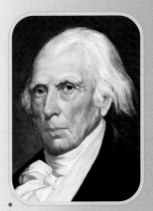

James Madison helped found today's Democratic Party.

JAMES MONROE

James Monroe (1758–1831) issued a famous statement during his presidency now called the Monroe Doctrine. It said that European countries should not try to take over any countries in the Western Hemisphere. Historians have called Monroe's presidency the Era of Good Feelings. This is because Americans began to feel more united and stronger as a country.

WILLIAM HENRY HARRISON

William Henry Harrison (1773–1841) was president for only one month. While giving his **inaugural** address, he caught a cold that turned into **pneumonia.** Harrison died on April 4, 1841.

JOHN TYLER

John Tyler (1790–1862) served in the U.S. House of Representatives and twice was governor of Virginia. In 1840, Tyler became the vice president to William Henry Harrison. When Harrison died, Tyler became the first vice president to take over for a president who had died.

ZACHARY TAYLOR

Zachary Taylor (1784–1850) was a career army officer who spent his military career fighting Native Americans and in the War with Mexico (1846–1848). He was nicknamed Old Rough and Ready because of his fighting ability.

Woodrow Wilson received the Nobel Peace Prize in 1919 for his work on the League of Nations.

WOODROW WILSON

Woodrow Wilson (1856–1924) attended the College of New Jersey (now Princeton University) and University of Virginia Law School. Later, he became a professor and president of Princeton. During his presidency, the United States fought in World War I (1914–1918). After the war, Wilson unsuccessfully tried to get the United States to join the League of Nations, which was the predecessor to the United Nations.

Virginia's Unique History

Virginia is the setting for major events in two of the most important periods in U.S. history—colonial America (1607–1783) and the **Civil War** (1861–1865). The event that started colonial America and the event that led to the end of colonial America both occurred within miles of each other in eastern Virginia. In addition, during the Civil War, Virginia was the main battleground. The North and South fought more battles in Virginia than in any other state.

Jamestown and Yorktown

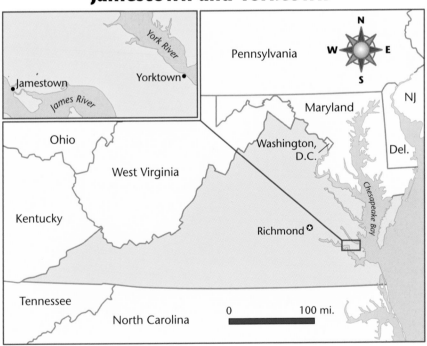

Jamestown and Yorktown are only about 20 miles from each other. These Virginia cities played an important role in early U.S. history.

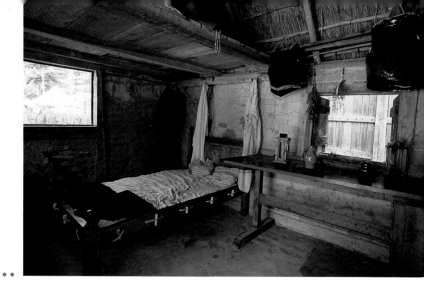

Jamestown Fort's wooden walls formed a triangle around a storehouse, church, and many houses. This photograph shows the inside of one of the houses.

JAMESTOWN

Colonial American history began in Jamestown, Virginia, on May 14, 1607—the day English colonists landed there. It was the location of the first permanent English settlement in North America. Colonists named the settlement after King James I of England. Today, Jamestown is a living museum that shows what life was like in Virginia in the 1600s. **Replicas** of the first ships to reach Jamestown are docked there. At Jamestown Fort and a Native American village, visitors can learn about the daily life of the first settlers and Native Americans. A museum displays **artifacts** from the settlement and the fort, including animal bones from food waste found in a pit dating from before 1610. These artifacts show that the people who landed at Jamestown ate mainly fish and turtles. Sturgeon was the most common fish.

YORKTOWN

The period of colonial America came to an end shortly after the defeat of

The Yorktown Victory Center features a Continental Army camp, where visitors can learn to fire Revolutionary War-era cannons.

British General Lord Cornwallis at Yorktown on October 19, 1781. The British defeat at Yorktown was the last major battle of the **Revolutionary War** (1775–1783). On that day, more than 8,000 British soldiers laid down their weapons and surrendered. After hearing news of the defeat, the British prime minister reportedly clutched his chest and screeched, "Oh God, it's all over." After two years of negotiations, Great Britain signed the Treaty of Paris, which recognized the independence of the United States.

VIRGINIA AND THE CIVIL WAR

The **Civil War** (1861–1865) was fought between the **Confederate** South and the Union states in the North. The Confederate states wanted to keep using slaves, to maintain their farming way of life, and to keep more power with individual states—called states' rights. The Union states were pushing for a more modern, industrial society and to end the expansion and existence of slavery.

Though the Civil War raged throughout most of the country, more than half of the war's 400-plus battles took place in Virginia. In addition, most of the South's great military leaders were Virginians, including Robert E. Lee, Stonewall Jackson, and the cavalry leader Jeb Stuart.

The Battle of Chancellorsville caused more than 24,000 casualties.

Major Battles of the Civil War in Virginia, 1861–1865

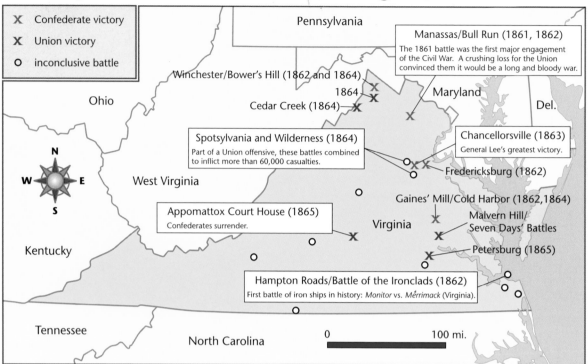

Legend:
- X Confederate victory
- X Union victory
- O inconclusive battle

Pennsylvania

Ohio

Maryland

Del.

West Virginia

Kentucky

Virginia

Tennessee

North Carolina

Winchester/Bower's Hill (1862 and 1864)
1864
Cedar Creek (1864)

Manassas/Bull Run (1861, 1862)
The 1861 battle was the first major engagement of the Civil War. A crushing loss for the Union convinced them it would be a long and bloody war.

Spotsylvania and Wilderness (1864)
Part of a Union offensive, these battles combined to inflict more than 60,000 casualties.

Chancellorsville (1863)
General Lee's greatest victory.

Fredericksburg (1862)

Appomattox Court House (1865)
Confederates surrender.

Gaines' Mill/Cold Harbor (1862, 1864)

Malvern Hill/Seven Days' Battles

Petersburg (1865)

Hampton Roads/Battle of the Ironclads (1862)
First battle of iron ships in history: *Monitor* vs. *Merrimack* (Virginia).

0   100 mi.

Because armies fought and marched across the state throughout the Civil War, Virginia's farms and towns suffered. The state of Virginia had a debt of about 42 million dollars after the war.

Virginia's geographic location, near Washington, D.C., and the fact that Richmond, Virginia, also served as the **Confederate** capital, guaranteed that Virginia would became a major battleground. By the end of the war, in April 1865, more than 26 major battles had taken place in Virginia. When Richmond fell in 1865, the end of the Civil War was near. Petersburg was the last line of defense for the **Confederate** capital. More than 30,000 Confederates are buried in Blandford Church cemetery in Petersburg.

Today, the church has been made into a memorial chapel for Confederate soldiers. The chapel includes fifteen stained glass windows dedicated to the soldiers. In addition, Petersburg National Battlefield and the National Museum of the Civil War are two sites that show camp life and the horrors of battle in the final days of the Civil War. The Museum of the Confederacy and the White House of the Confederacy, in Richmond, have a collection of more than 15,000 **artifacts** from the Civil War.

ARLINGTON NATIONAL CEMETERY

The great Confederate general Robert E. Lee and his wife Mary Anna lived in a **mansion** on 1,100 acres of the Arlington **Plantation** in Virginia. It overlooked Washington, D.C. When the Civil War broke out, the Lees left, and the federal government took over the mansion and grounds. In 1864, the plantation was turned into a military cemetery. Today, more than 250,000 soldiers are buried in Arlington National Cemetery. In addition, other important figures are buried there, including two U.S. presidents, eleven Supreme Court **Justices,** and some of the country's astronauts. More than four million people visit the cemetery every year.

William Henry Christman, a member of the 67th Pennsylvania Infantry, was the first person buried in Arlington National Cemetery, on May 13, 1864.

The Tomb of the Unknown Soldier in Arlington National Cemetery holds the remains of more than 5,000 unknown soldiers.

Sports in Virginia

Virginia sports fans support a wide variety of minor league sports, Virginia college teams, **NASCAR** drivers, and professional tennis players and golfers.

CAR RACING

Virginia's biggest single spectator sporting event is car racing. Thousands of fans visit speedways in Martinsville and Richmond to cheer for their favorite NASCAR drivers. The Martinsville Speedway opened in 1947, two years before the founding of NASCAR. It holds such races as the Virginia 500 and can hold more than 86,000 spectators. The Richmond International Raceway began hosting races on dirt in 1946. It was finally paved in 1968. Today, the raceway has a capacity of more than 105,000 people. Ricky Rudd, Elliott Sadler, Ward and Jeff Burton, Stacy Compton, and Hermie Sadler are only a few of the successful Virginia racecar drivers.

Wendell Scott

Wendell Scott of Danville, Virginia, was the first African American to compete in the all-white sport of stock car racing in 1952. Scott was the Virginia state stock-car-racing champion in 1959.

Virginia's Professional Teams

The Richmond Braves are part of minor league baseball's International League (IL). The Richmond Braves develop players for Major League Baseball's Atlanta Braves. Richmond and Atlanta have the second longest partnership in minor league baseball. They have been working together since 1966. Famous Richmond ballplayers include such current greats as Tom Glavine, Chipper Jones, and John Smoltz. Richmond has put together eighteen winning seasons, including five regular season titles and four league championships. Other Virginia minor league teams include the Norfolk Tides, the Lynchburg Hillcats, the Potomac Cannons, and the Salem Avalanche.

Richmond Braves outfielder Ozzie Timmons looks for the next pitch.

College Sports

College sports offer fans in Virginia many opportunities for sporting excellence. Virginia Tech, in Blacksburg, has enjoyed recent success in football. It won the conference title in 1995, 1996, and 1999. It also played for the national championship in the 2000 Sugar Bowl. The University of Virginia, in Charlottesville, excels in men's soccer. It has won five national championships since 1989. Since the mid-1970s, Old Dominion University (ODU), in Norfolk, has won twelve national championships, including nine in field hockey. The ODU women's basketball team has won three national championships. Nancy Lieberman-Cline, an ODU basketball

Secretariat

Secretariat, one of the greatest **thoroughbreds** of all time, was born at Meadow Farms Stables in Caroline County, Virginia. Secretariat won the **Triple Crown** in 1973 and set an all-time record for the 1-mile race at 1 minute, 59 seconds. ESPN Television named Secretariat the 35th greatest athlete of the 1900s.

star, was one of the first women basketball players to play professionally. She was also on the 1976 U.S. Olympic Team that won a silver medal and helped ODU to two national titles in 1979 and 1980.

Besides being a great tennis player, Arthur Ashe also wrote a history of African-American athletes called A Hard Road to Glory.

GOLF AND TENNIS

Virginians have also excelled in golf and tennis. Born near Hot Springs, Virginia, Sam Snead claimed he never had a golf lesson. Nevertheless, his 81 Professional Golfer's Association (PGA) tournament victories give him more than any other golfer. He also won every major tournament, except for the U.S. Open, in which he finished second four times. In 1965, Snead, at 52 years of age, was the oldest golfer ever to win a PGA event. Another great Virginia golfer, Curtis Strange, was born in Norfolk. He has seventeen PGA tour wins as well as back-to-back U.S. Open championships in 1988 and 1989.

Tennis great Arthur Ashe grew up in Richmond. He is the only African-American male to win a major tennis title. He won the U.S. Open in 1968, the Australian Open in 1970, and Wimbledon in 1975. He also won 30 other singles titles. Ashe was a person of strong character who overcame many racial barriers. He opened the world of tennis to African Americans by never giving up his dream to compete.

Arts in Virginia

Theater, art, and music are important to Virginians. This importance shows in the variety of Virginia **cultural** options.

PERFORMING ARTS AND THEATER

Wolf Trap is the nation's National Park for the Performing Arts. Virginia is the only state in the country that has a national park built just for the arts. Wolf Trap is a 130-acre park located in northern Virginia, near Vienna. Concerts, symphonies, plays, dances, and other performances take place there year round.

The state theater of Virginia is the Barter Theatre of Abington, Virginia. Started in 1933 by a group of New York actors, the Barter Theatre is one of the country's oldest professional theaters. It was named the Barter Theatre because at one time people paid for tickets with milk, ham, chicken, and other food. Trading goods and

Virginians and tourists have been enjoying shows at Wolf Trap since it opened in 1966.

Barter Theatre has two "By Kids, For Kids" productions each year, the first for ages twelve through eighteen, and the second for ages six through eleven.

services in such a way is called bartering. Two of the most unusual items bartered were a live hog and a dead rattlesnake. Today, the Barter celebrates its heritage by accepting donations for an area food bank for at least one performance a year. Barter's famous past performers include Gregory Peck, Ernest Borgnine, Ned Beatty, and Larry Linville.

ART MUSEUMS

Visitors can take a trip around the world and journey through time by visiting the Virginia Museum of Fine Arts in Richmond. It is filled with original art from Europe, North America, and Asia. Treasures from ancient Egypt, Greece, Rome, and the Americas include 6,000-year-old Egyptian mummies and Greek and Roman pottery.

The Chrysler Museum of Art is located in Norfolk. It features European and American collections of sculp-

The Virginia Museum of Fine Arts has a famous collection of painted and jeweled eggs by Peter Carl Fabergé, which were originally made for rulers of Russia.

tures, paintings, and photographs. The Chrysler Museum has more than 30,000 objects in its collection, which covers about 5,000 years of world history. The museum also has one of the world's great collections of glass, including many works by Louis Comfort Tiffany.

Virginia Music

Virginia has a strong tradition of bluegrass, country, and jazz music. European settlers brought songs and tales to the southern Appalachian region in the 1900s. These songs and stories became the roots of country and bluegrass music.

Each year in the second week of August, the city of Galax in western Virginia holds its Old Fiddler's Convention. Musicians and country music fans from around the world travel to Galax to perform and hear the music of the Blue Ridge Mountains.

Jazz has its roots in African-American and gospel music. Pearl Bailey (1918–1990) was a great jazz singer. She was born in Newport News and learned to sing in the local church where her father was the minister. Bailey was a singer and performer all of her life. Another great jazz musician was Charlie Byrd (1925–1999). He was born in Chuckatuck, Virginia, and grew up listening to visitors who played music in his father's general store. He became a famous classical and jazz guitarist whose music is known all over the world.

Musicians perform at the Old Fiddler's Convention in Galax.

Virginia's Food

Good food has been part of Virginia **culture** for a long time. Peanuts and ham are two of the state's most famous foods. Virginia hams were prepared at Jamestown as early as the 1600s. Peanuts arrived on colonial trading ships and later became an important farm crop.

SMITHFIELD HAM

Queen Victoria (1819–1901) of England loved Smithfield hams and had six delivered to her cooks every day. They were once produced from hogs raised on a diet of acorns, hickory nuts, and peanuts. Peanuts are still a part of the hogs' diet. The hams are smoked for six months to two years. The resulting ham is rich, salty, and dry. Smithfield hams are shipped all over the world.

Smithfield hams are slowly smoked using oak, hickory, and apple woods, which add to the unique flavor.

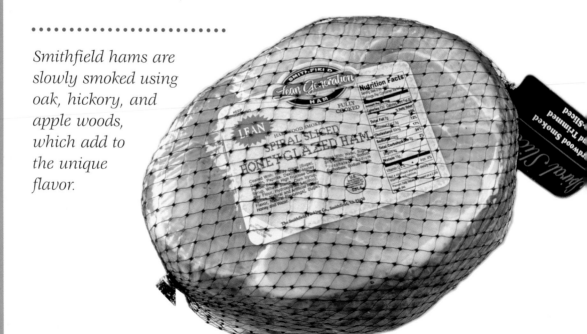

Sugar-Coated Peanuts

You can try this recipe for a tasty treat using peanuts grown in Virginia:

Ingredients:

1 cup granulated sugar

1/2 cup water

2 cups raw shelled peanuts,
    with the skins on

Directions:

Dissolve the sugar in water in a saucepan over medium heat. Add the peanuts and continue to cook over medium heat, stirring frequently. Cook the mixture until the peanuts are completely sugared (coated with no syrup left). Pour the peanuts onto an ungreased cookie sheet and then separate the peanuts with a fork. Bake the peanuts at 300°F for approximately 30 minutes, stirring every 10 minutes. Allow the peanuts to cool and store them in an airtight container. This recipe makes about 1.5 pounds of peanuts.

PEANUTS

Peanut pie, peanut brittle, peanut butter, peanut soup, and peanut butter cookies are all made with peanuts, of course. **Civil War** soldiers from the South called peanuts goober peas and even made up marching songs about them. **Confederate** soldiers' food consisted mainly of peanuts by the end of the war. In 1906, Planters Peanut Company, located in Suffolk, Virginia, was the first company to roast shelled peanuts in oil.

Virginia's Folklore and Legends

One of the most mysterious places in Virginia is the Great Dismal Swamp. Particular stones at Fairy Stone State Park also provide some entertaining **folktales.**

THE GREAT DISMAL SWAMP

Lake Drummond, a 3,100-acre lake, is located in the center of the Great Dismal Swamp. Some scientists think a giant meteor may have formed the lake when it struck the earth thousands of years ago. Others think that a **peat** fire burned out the depression that forms the shallow lake. Ancient cypress trees reach up out of the water and mark the rim of the lake. The Spanish moss that hangs from some of these trees gives the swamp an unusual look. Strange, spooky lights are often seen in the swamp at night. Scientists believe they are caused by the natural decay of wood and **fungi.**

Visitors to the Great Dismal Swamp can enjoy hiking, biking, fishing, and boating. But be careful, because three types of poisonous snakes live here—the cottonmouth, canebrake rattler, and copperhead.

For many years, people believed these little stone crosses protected the wearer against sickness, accidents, and disasters.

LEGEND OF THE FAIRY STONE

The Legend of the Fairy Stone is a folktale explaining how the crosslike stones found at Fairy Stone State Park came to be. According to the story, many hundreds of years ago fairies were dancing around a spring of water when a messenger arrived from a city far away, bringing news of the death of **Jesus Christ.** When these creatures of the forest heard the story, they wept. As their tears fell upon the earth, they formed crosses. When the fairies disappeared from the enchanted place, the ground around the spring and the nearby valley was covered with these crosses, which are reminders of the event. The crosslike stones are actually staurolite crystals, which form naturally in the shape of a cross.

The Deer Tree

A knotted bald cypress tree along the edge of Lake Drummond is shaped like a deer. One legend says that a deer was escaping hunters and magically turned itself into a tree. Another legend says that the deer was a witch who made fun of hunting dogs. She ran into the swamp in the form of a deer to escape the dogs and turned herself into a tree. However, she was then unable to turn herself back into a witch or into a deer.

Virginia's Businesses and Products

Through much of its history, Virginia's economy has relied on farming. Today, however, manufacturing and the federal government anchor the state's economy.

SHIPBUILDING

Newport News Shipbuilding (NNS) has more than 16,000 employees and is the world's largest private shipbuilding yard. In 1891, NNS finished its first ship, a tugboat named *Dorothy.* Since that time, NNS has built more than 700 ships, including nearly 30 U.S. Navy aircraft carriers. They are the largest warships in the world, weighing over 90,000 tons each. NNS also built three natural gas tankers. Each ship weighs more than 390,000 tons, the largest ever built in the United States.

GOVERNMENT JOBS

Because Virginia borders Washington, D.C., many federal agencies and departments are located in Virginia. About 25 percent of

Newport News Shipbuilding has been designing, building, and repairing ships for over 100 years. The company also builds nuclear-powered submarines for the U.S. Navy.

Virginia's workers work for the U.S. government. The largest state agency, the Department of Defense, is located in Arlington. Its headquarters, called the Pentagon,

The Pentagon has three times the floor space of the Empire State Building, in New York City, and the U.S. Capitol could fit into any one of the five sections.

employs about 23,000 people. These people help to plan and carry out the defense of the United States. Some jobs, such as those on the 230-person restaurant staff, service the Pentagon employees. Pentagon workers drink 4,500 cups of coffee, 1,700 pints of milk, and 6,800 soft drinks each day. Other federal employers in Virginia include the Central Intelligence Agency, near McLean; Marine Corps Base Quantico; Norfolk Naval Base; and Langley Air Force Base.

Major Virginia Companies

Company	Location	Employees
1. Circuit City Stores, Inc.	Richmond	50,500
2. CSX Corp. (train freight)	Richmond	48,950
3. Smithfield Foods, Inc.	Smithfield	30,800
4. AMF Bowling, Inc.	Richmond	15,568
5. Eskimo Pie Corp.	Richmond	105

Attractions and Landmarks

SHENANDOAH NATIONAL PARK

Located just an hour's drive from Washington, D.C., Shenandoah National Park is a wilderness of nearly 200,000 acres. In 1926, Congress voted to build the park in the Blue Ridge Mountains. Unique features of the park include the Appalachian Trail and Skyline Drive. The Appalachian Trail is a trail that extends from Mount Katahdin, in Maine, to Springer Mountain, in Georgia. About 101 miles of the trail are in Shenandoah National Park. While hiking this trail, you might encounter such animals as deer, black bears, and wild turkeys. Skyline Drive was built in the 1930s. It winds for 105 miles along the park's mountain tops across the length of the park. It provides views of the landscape to the east and west. The drive eventually connects with the Blue Ridge Parkway.

The last section of the Blue Ridge Parkway was completed in 1987, which was 52 years after the project started.

Virginia State Parks and Natural Wonders

0   100 mi.

N W E S

♠ State/Regional Park
▭ National Park

Winchester•
Potomac River
•Arlington

Harrisonburg•
Natural Chimneys ♠
Shenandoah Shenandoah River
Shenandoah National Park
Lake Anna SP ♠
Staunton• ♠
Luray Caverns •
Charlottesville•
Mattaponi River
Rappahannock R.
Pamunkey River
Natural Bridge •♠
James River
☼Richmond
York River
Chesapeake Bay
Salem •
Blacksburg• •Roanoke
Claytor Lake
Smith Mountain Lake
Roanoke
Nottoway River
Newport News•
First Landing SP ♠
Cumberland Gap |
Clinch River
New River
Roanoke River
♠ Philpott Lake
♠ Fairy Stone SP
John H. Kerr Reservoir
Shot Tower State Historical Park

BLUE RIDGE PARKWAY

The Blue Ridge Mountains are named for the hazy blue color they reflect when seen from a distance. Through the Blue Ridge Mountains runs the Blue Ridge Parkway. It connects the southern end of Shenandoah National Park with the Great Smoky Mountains in North Carolina. The 469-mile parkway is the most visited place in the national park system. Construction on the road began in 1935. More than 700 million visitors have traveled the Blue Ridge Parkway since its opening.

Virginia's state park system is unique in the fact that it is the only one in the United States to have opened six parks on a single day, June 15, 1936.

CUMBERLAND GAP

The Cumberland Gap was cut into the eastern United States by streams. It is located near the point where Kentucky, Virginia, and Tennessee meet. The gap was named for the duke of Cumberland, son of the English King George II. It became a main road through the mountains. It also helped to open the **Northwest Territory** to settlement and allowed for the western boundary of the Thirteen Colonies to extend to the Mississippi River. In 1940, 32 square miles of the Cumberland area were set aside as the Cumberland Gap National Historical Park.

Virginians and tourists alike enjoy the ocean in Virginia Beach.

VIRGINIA'S STATE PARKS

Virginia's state park system is the oldest in the country. Virginia opened its system with six parks on June 15, 1936. First Landing State Park was one of its first state parks. It includes beaches and dunes, as well as a bald cypress swamp. English settlers landed on its beaches in 1607, one month before they settled at Jamestown.

Another park, Shot Tower Historical State Park, contains one of only three shot towers still standing in the United States. A shot tower was used to make shots, or musket balls. This tower is more than 150 years old. **Molten** lead was taken to the top of this 75-foot tower and poured into a shaft buried another 75 feet into the ground. As the lead fell, it formed balls small enough to use in muskets. The balls then collected in a kettle of water to harden.

NATURAL WONDERS

Natural Bridge has been called one of the seven natural wonders of the world. The stone bridge was created when water wore away the soft rock and left a bridge of hard rock. It is more than 100

After Jefferson bought the land including Natural Bridge, he built a log cabin near the site for guests. European visitors were very interested in this natural wonder.

million years old. Natural Bridge stands 215 feet tall and is 90 feet wide.

The deepest caverns in the eastern United States are located near Natural Bridge. They descend about 900 feet into the ground. They were discovered in 1891 but were not opened to the public until 1977.

Seven ancient rock formations rise 120 feet above the North River in the Shenandoah Valley. From some places they look like chimneys and from others they look like castle ruins. The formations, called Natural Chimneys, were shaped by the wearing away of limestone over many thousands of years.

LURAY CAVERNS

Luray Caverns in the Shenandoah Valley has great **stalactites** and **stalagmites.** Stalactites form from **minerals** in dripping water and hang from the ceilings of caves. Stalagmites form when the mineral crystals build up from the floor. This mineral buildup makes columns, frozen waterfalls, and other formations. The National Park Service and the U.S. Department of the Interior made Luray Caverns a registered natural **landmark** because of its natural formations.

Luray Caverns is known for its variety of formations and color. Some rooms are large, with ten-story-high ceilings, stone columns, and clear pools of water.

MARITIME MUSEUMS

Ships and sailing are an important and large part of Virginia's history. The battleship USS *Wisconsin* found a home at Nauticus, the National Maritime Center in Norfolk. There, people can visit the *Wisconsin* and learn about life on the ship and its important role in World War II (1939–1945).

The center also contains the Hampton Roads Naval Museum, the National Oceanic Atmospheric Administration (NOAA), and the tugboat *Huntington,* which is a tugboat museum. The NOAA researches and gathers information about the oceans, the atmosphere, space, and the sun. It uses this information to warn of dangerous weather. It also charts the seas and skies and guides the use and protection of the ocean and coastal areas.

Besides seeing some amazing ships, visitors to the National Maritime Center can learn about the modern U.S. Navy, how weather reports are made, and what kinds of sea creatures live in the Chesapeake Bay.

NAUTICUS

The Governor's Palace in Williamsburg was the home of British royal governors from 1714 to 1775.

COLONIAL WILLIAMSBURG

Colonial Williamsburg was the location of Virginia's second capital in 1699. Jamestown, Virginia's first capital, burned in 1698. The historic area of Williamsburg centers on the Duke of Gloucester Street. At one end of the street is the old **capitol** building and at the other end is the College of William and Mary, founded in 1693. Historic taverns, stores, merchants, offices, and homes of the 1700s line the street between them. Williamsburg still contains 88 original structures.

APPOMATTOX COURT HOUSE

Appomattox Court House National Historic Park shows where the **Civil War** (1861–1865) ended. General Robert E. Lee, the main commander of the Confederate army, surrendered to Ulysses S. Grant, commander of Union forces, in the McLean home on April 9, 1865. The McLeans lived in the town of Appomattox Court House at the time, and it was the only suitable site in the area for the surrender. The national historic park includes about 1,800 acres of rolling hills in central Virginia, the McLean home, and the village of Appomattox Court House. The U.S. government designated it a National Historical Park on April 15, 1954.

Buildings and Structures of Virginia

Virginia has many unique buildings, some dating back hundreds of years. Some of the notable buildings include George Washington's Mount Vernon home and Thomas Jefferson's house, called Monticello.

MOUNT VERNON

Mount Vernon is one of the most famous homes in the United States. It is located on the banks of the Potomac River near Washington, D.C. Mount Vernon was Washington's home for more than 45 years. He **inherited** it upon the death of his brother Lawrence's widow in 1761.

University of Virginia

Thomas Jefferson's dream was to build a college near his home in Monticello. He wanted to create a school where learning would take place in an **"academical** village." He designed the buildings, which still stand in Charlottesville, to reflect his vision. The University of Virginia, in Charlottesville, opened its doors in 1825.

Mount Vernon is made of pine but is rusticated—a treatment that gives it the appearance of stone.

Lawrence named the property Mount Vernon after his commanding officer Admiral Edward Vernon of the British Navy.

When Washington inherited the house, it had four rooms, a central hall on the first floor, and three bedrooms on the second. Washington raised the house to two-and-a-half stories and redecorated the interior. He also added north and south wings and a large dining room. Washington himself designed the two-story outdoor balcony overlooking the Potomac River and the Maryland shore. Washington also added a **cupola.**

At the time of Washington's death, in 1799, Mount Vernon included more than 8,000 acres and five farms. After the White House, it is the most visited historic home in the United States.

Chesapeake Bay Bridge-Tunnel

The Chesapeake Bay Bridge-Tunnel is one of the Seven Engineering Wonders of the Modern World. The 17.6-mile combination bridge and tunnel connects Cape Charles of the Eastern Shore to the Southside cities of Virginia Beach and Norfolk.

In Jefferson's day, Monticello was heated by its eight fireplaces. Candles provided light, but Jefferson also owned oil-burning lamps.

MONTICELLO

Monticello, located on a small mountain near Charlottesville, means "little mountain" in Italian. The house has a central three-story frame with a wing on either side. The kitchen, laundry room, servants' quarters, and other buildings are hidden beneath two long L-shaped terraces. Jefferson connected the terraces to the basement of the main house with an underground passage.

Jefferson also added such practical elements as a revolving desk and a bed that opened onto both his bedroom and study. Today, Monticello is recognized as an international treasure. It is the only house in the United States on the United Nations's list of protected sites.

Inside Monticello

Thomas Jefferson was an innovator. He liked to improve practical gadgets. He had a clock connected to a seven-day calendar that marked off the days as different weights made it run. He built mechanical doors to the parlor. The movement of one door automatically opened the other by use of a machine hidden beneath

the floor. Jefferson built mechanical lifts called **dumbwaiters** in the dining room. The dumbwaiters could be used to send wine bottles up to the dining room from the cellar below.

Map of Virginia

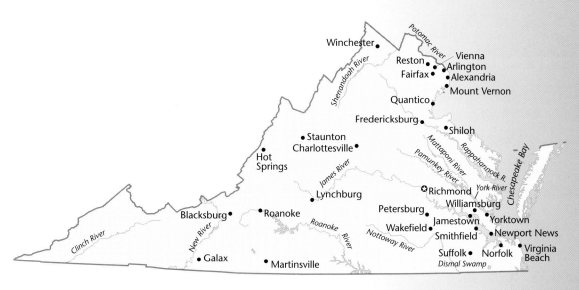

Winchester

Potomac River

Shenandoah River

Reston
Fairfax
Vienna
Arlington
Alexandria
Mount Vernon

Quantico

Fredericksburg

Shiloh

Staunton
Charlottesville

Hot Springs

James River

Mattaponi River

Pamunkey River

Rappahannock R.

Chesapeake Bay

Lynchburg

Richmond

York River

Williamsburg

Petersburg

Jamestown
Yorktown

Blacksburg

Roanoke

New River

Roanoke River

Wakefield

Smithfield

Newport News

Nottoway River

Suffolk
Norfolk
Virginia Beach

Clinch River

Galax

Martinsville

Dismal Swamp

CANADA

ME
VT NH
NY MA
CT RI
PA NJ
MD DE
OH
IN
WV
KY Virginia
TN NC
SC
AL GA
FL
MI

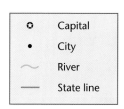

✪	Capital
•	City
～	River
—	State line

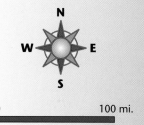

N
W E
S

0   100 mi.

Glossary

academical word that describes something that has to do with schools and learning

appeal legal process in which a ruling by a lower court is reviewed by a higher court

artifact object remaining from a particular time

cabinet group of persons who act as advisors

capitol official building in which lawmakers meet. *Capitol,* with an *o,* refers to the building. *Capital,* with an *a,* refers to a city.

civil war war between groups of citizens of the same country. The states in the North and the states in the South fought each other from 1861 to 1865 in the U.S. Civil War.

commonwealth state or other political unit founded on law and united by an agreement of the people for the common good

Confederacy the eleven states that separated from the Union in 1861. The word *Confederate* describes something related to the Confederacy.

culture the arts, beliefs, values, and customs of a group of people

cupola rounded dome with a circular base that forms a ceiling

Declaration of Independence document that announced that the American colonies were no longer willing to be ruled by Great Britain

delegate person who represents a group

descendant one who comes down from a particular ancestor

dominion territory under the control of a ruler

dumbwaiter small elevator for carrying food, dishes, or other small items from one floor to another

estuary place where the sea and a river meet

folklore customs, stories, dances, or art forms preserved among a particular people

folktale story told by many people, usually by spoken word

fossil remains of an ancient living thing, usually turned to stone

fungus living things that are neither plants nor animals. Mushrooms and molds are fungi.

inaugural the first time

inherit receive by legal right from a person after his or her death

Jesus Christ founder of the Christian religion

justice judge

landmark building or object that is important for its historical value, its beauty, or some other quality

lieutenant governor person who is second in command to the governor

mace fancy club carried before certain officials as a sign of authority

mansion large house of a wealthy person

mineral solid substance formed in the earth by nature and obtained by mining

molten melted by heat

NASCAR National Association of Stock Car Auto Racing

Northwest Territory huge area of what is now the United States. It included what are now the states of Ohio, Indiana, Illinois, Michigan, Wisconsin, and part of Minnesota.

peat type of fuel formed naturally from plants. Peat is a stage in the formation of coal.

plantation large farm in the south for growing crops such as tobacco

pneumonia disease caused by an infection to the lungs

predator something that hunts other animals

prosperity succeed or flourish

replica copy of something

representative government government of lawmakers elected to represent the citizens

Revolutionary War war that the Thirteen Colonies fought from 1775 to 1783 for independence from Great Britain

rotunda circular building or room that usually is covered with a dome

self-government government by action of the people who make up the community

stalactite deposit hanging from the roof or side of a cave in the shape of an icicle formed by minerals in dripping water

stalagmite deposit like an upside down stalactite formed by the dripping of water containing minerals onto the floor of a cave

survey inspect or examine for condition or value

term length of time an elected official spends in office

thoroughbred type of racehorse

Triple Crown horse racing title won by a three-year-old horse that wins the Kentucky Derby, the Preakness, and the Belmont Stakes

tyrant ruler who is cruel and harsh

More Books to Read

Fradin, Dennis Brindell. *Virginia: From Sea to Shining Sea.* Danbury, Conn.: Scholastic Library Publishing, 2000.

Heinrichs, Ann. *Virginia.* Minnetonka, Minn.: Compass Point Books, 2002.

Marsh, Carole. *My First Pocket Guide Virginia.* Peachtree City, Ga.: Gallopade International, 2001.

McAuliffe, Bill. *Virginia Facts and Symbols.* Danbury, Conn.: Scholastic Library Publishing, 2000.

Index

About the Author

Karla Smith grew up in a navy family and moved several times before settling down in Suffolk, Virginia. She has been teaching third, fourth, and fifth graders social studies since 1969. When she is not teaching, Smith enjoys exploring Virginia's waters in a sailboat.